Trackers

Teacher's Guide

Bear

Trackers

Starter

KATE RUTTLE

Series Editor

OXFORD

UNIVERSITY PRESS

OXFORD
UNIVERSITY PRESS

Great Clarendon Street, Oxford OX2 6DP

Oxford University Press is a department of the University of Oxford.
It furthers the University's objective of excellence in research, scholarship,
and education by publishing worldwide in

Oxford   New York

Auckland   Cape Town   Dar es Salaam   Hong Kong   Karachi
Kuala Lumpur   Madrid   Melbourne   Mexico City   Nairobi
New Delhi   Shanghai   Taipei   Toronto

With offices in

Argentina   Austria   Brazil   Chile   Czech Republic   France   Greece
Guatemala   Hungary   Italy   Japan   Poland   Portugal   Singapore
South Korea   Switzerland   Thailand   Turkey   Ukraine   Vietnam

Oxford is a registered trade mark of Oxford University Press
in the UK and in certain other countries

Text copyright © Kate Ruttle 2005

The moral rights of the author have been asserted

Database right Oxford University Press (maker)

First published 2005

British Library Cataloguing in Publication Data

Data available

ISBN-13: 978-0-19-8384830
ISBN-10: 0-19-8384831

10 9 8 7 6 5 4 3 2

Illustrations by Jane Bottomley

Typeset by Fakenham Photosetting, Fakenham, Norfolk

Printed by Ashford Colour Press, Gosport, Hants

Acknowledgements

As authors of the *Trackers* series, we would like to thank the many 'behind the scenes' people who
have worked so hard to make this project such fun. In particular we owe thanks to the talented and
industrious team at Oxford University Press whose enthusiasm and dedication to all aspects of the
project has been unwavering and infectious. We are also extremely grateful for the skill and hard
work of the freelance people we have been lucky enough to work with, in particular to Jenny Roberts,
who edited all of the books.

Trackers has been trialled in many different schools around England and we are grateful for all the
enthusiastic feedback from the teachers and children as well as those of our invaluable reviewers.
Thank you everybody for your comments. We have read and discussed them all and your feedback
has helped us to make the books even better!

Sarah Fleming, Paul Shipton and Kate Ruttle

Contents

Introduction

The *Trackers* series of books is a carefully structured non-fiction and fiction reading resource for children aged 7+ who have a reading age of 5+. The books are particularly suitable for children who:

★ are finding reading a struggle,
★ are reluctant to read, or
★ are acquiring English as an additional language.

The two main aims of *Trackers* are:

★ to provide motivating 'must read' books with an interest age of 7+ and which matches the conceptual development of these children, while having a reading age of 5+;
★ to develop children's comprehension skills through generating an expectation that reading is concerned with 'getting meaning off the page', using a variety of strategies and cueing systems.

Trackers components and levels

Trackers level	National Curriculum level	Interest age	Pupil reading books	Teaching material
Starter Bear tracks	England & Wales – within level 1C Scotland – working towards level A N. Ireland – within level 1	Interest age 7+ years	6 non-ficton (16pp) 4 Space School Stories (16pp) 2 variety fiction (16pp)	Starter Teacher's Guide Teacher's Guide for Variety Fiction (for all levels) Guided Reading Booklet for every title
1 Elephant tracks	England & Wales – 1B Scotland – working within level A N. Ireland – working towards level 2	7+ years	6 non-fiction (16pp) 4 Space School Stories (16pp) 2 variety fiction (16pp)	Teacher's Guide for levels 1 and 2
2 Frog tracks	England & Wales – 1A/B Scotland – working within level A N. Ireland – working towards level 2	7+ years	6 non-fiction (16pp) 4 Space School Stories (16pp) 2 variety fiction (16pp)	Guided Reading Booklet for every title
3 Giraffe tracks	England & Wales – 1A Scotland – working towards level B N. Ireland – working within level 2	8+ years	6 non-fiction (16pp) 4 Space School Stories (16pp) 2 variety fiction (16pp)	Teacher's Guide for levels 3 and 4
4 Parrot tracks	England & Wales – 1A/2C Scotland – working towards level B N. Ireland – working within level 2	8+ years	6 non-fiction (24pp) 4 Space School Stories (24pp) 2 variety fiction (24pp)	Guided Reading Booklet for every title
5 Tiger tracks	England & Wales – 2C Scotland – working within level B N. Ireland – working within level 2	9+ years	6 non-fiction (24pp) 4 Space School Stories (24pp) 2 variety fiction (24pp)	Teacher's Guide for levels 5 and 6
6 Zebra tracks	England & Wales – 2B Scotland – working within level B N. Ireland – working within level 2	9+ years	6 non-fiction (24pp) 4 Space School Stories (24pp) 2 variety fiction (24pp)	Guided Reading Booklet for every title

How do Trackers differ from books designed for younger children?

By the time children are 7+, they will have had previous experience of reading, albeit not always successful. This means that *Trackers* can make assumptions that children understand how reading 'works' (for example the eye-movement is from left to right across the page; book language has its own conventions; readers have different expectations of fiction and non-fiction books). *Trackers* books differ from books whose target audience is children aged 4+ in a number of key ways:

★ All the books look like books for older children; they are not printed in a large font with very simple illustrations but have age appropriate illustrations and are printed in a variety of appropriately sized typefaces.

★ *Trackers* books are designed to grab the reader's attention and to make the children want to read and re-read them. Given that many children in the target audience have not found reading to be a rewarding experience, *Trackers* books work extra hard to provide that added incentive.

★ The design of each book is varied to suit the contents of the book. This is consistent with other books in the 7+ classroom.

★ The non-fiction books look like other non-fiction books available in school and class libraries. For instance, they make use of more sophisticated presentation devices like simple charts, graphs and tables, and the text is not in the same place on all pages.

★ The non-fiction books include real, 'new' information that is age appropriate. Many non-fiction books for younger children won't add to older children's general knowledge – *Trackers* will!

★ The fiction story lines are more sophisticated than those used in the early stages of 'traditional' reading schemes and are aimed at the more mature humour and understanding of the slightly older child.

★ The books are longer than comparable books in traditional reading schemes and there is more text on the page. Since we are providing books for older children, the traditional eight-page 'small books for small hands' approach is unnecessary, as is the idea that there should only be one line of text on a page. If the text is accessible and interesting, older children can cope with two or three lines of text, even in the very earliest stages, and often need this quantity of text to give a good 'run in' so that comprehension strategies will work.

Are different Trackers titles aimed at children in particular year groups?

No. *Trackers* are aimed at any child aged between about 7 and 12 whose reading attainment matches the book. The reading profile on page 48 will give more guidance as to which *Trackers* level a child is best suited for, but readership is intended to be determined by reading attainment, not chronological age.

Do Trackers support the National Literacy Strategy and the National Curriculum in England and Wales?

Yes. Although none of the books is specifically linked to particular reading objectives (in order that they are not seen to be directed at any particular age group) the texts are carefully written to be rich enough in both language and content for age-appropriate discussions and investigations. The Key Stage 2 and 3 objectives in the NLS (National Literacy Strategy) have been borne in mind both in the texts and in the Guided Reading Booklets which accompany each text.

The non-fiction text types chosen for *Trackers* are those specified most commonly in the *NLS Framework* and the topics are all relevant to the National Curriculum and to the QCA programmes of study. Specific cross-curricular links are suggested for each book and page 11 contains suggestions for integrating the books into class topics and projects. Many of these suggestions are consistent with the Literacy Across the Curriculum advice given to Key Stage 3 teachers.

Do Trackers support the Education 5–14 guidelines in Scotland and the National Curriculum in Northern Ireland?

Yes. All the *Trackers* titles have been checked by an expert in Scotland and do support the guidelines, both in literacy and across the wider curriculum. Again, no specific references and objectives are shown, but expected learning outcomes are made explicit.

Do Trackers *help to accelerate reading ability?*

Yes, in two main ways:

★ *By promoting age-appropriate reading skills*

Children aged 7+ who struggle with reading tend to experience difficulty across the curriculum because information and resources are increasingly delivered through the written word. Many children who find reading hard are otherwise capable of accessing an age-appropriate curriculum and these children need to develop 'book awareness' understanding (e.g. how non-fiction books are organised; how authors create characters and settings) in order that they can track the progress made by their peers.

★ *By challenging children to try to read slightly more complex language*

All **Trackers** books have two levels of text: the main text which is very structured (see pages 9 and 10) and additional 'secondary' text which is slightly more challenging. Experience shows that most of the children who could read the main text in a book were eager to attempt the more challenging secondary text and they were often successful. There is less secondary text in the *Bear tracks* books than at other levels, to avoid the pages looking too busy.

What is the difference between 'main text' and 'secondary text'?

Main text: The main text in each book is carefully structured to promote gradual, secure progression through the development of different skills and strategies for reading (see page 7). In the non-fiction books, this text is always clearly marked by some design device that is identified on the inside front cover of each book. If children only read the main text in any book, the book will make complete sense and be a satisfying read.

The main text is intended to be at the child's instructional level (i.e. they can read about 90 – 95% independently and accurately). This is the text children should work at independently in guided reading sessions.

The main text is used to calculate the word count, phonic focus and high frequency words for each book.

Secondary text: In all the books, there is additional text whose purpose varies depending on the text type or genre. In fiction the secondary text is in speech bubbles or environmental print. The secondary text is usually at the level above the main text, so when the children move to the next level of **Trackers** they will be well prepared for its challenges.

This secondary text has three main functions:

★ to offer an additional level of challenge which encourages children to try to stretch their reading abilities within a secure and motivating context;

★ to give additional information which increases the readership of the book and the understanding and enjoyment of each reader;

★ to provide age-appropriate book features which can be mediated by an adult to help to develop the children's age-appropriate reading behaviours and understanding.

In the non-fiction, some features are consistently counted as secondary text in all text types. These include:

★ *all the organisational features of the books* (contents page, headings, glossaries, blurb): It is expected that these features will primarily be used in the context of an adult teaching the children to use these features efficiently and correctly to find information. Most of the words used for headings, etc. are 'content' words which are easily read in the context of the pictures and the on-going text, but which are not expected to be read in isolation. Since they are read with an adult, glossaries and indexes include words from the secondary text throughout the book.

★ *the 'look back' section:* Many of the non-fiction books include a 'look back' section which encourages children to revisit the book to find specific information. Again, it is anticipated that this activity will be mediated by an adult, so the 'look back' section is secondary text.

Text types and genres

Trackers includes books from a range of text types and genres because they present different reading challenges and offer opportunities for teaching a variety of reading strategies (including, for instance: a range of purposes for reading, a variety of comprehension strategies and different strategies for decoding print). The language conventions for each different text type also varies, and this is reflected in the overall word count.

Fiction

Trackers level	Number of words	Number of pages	Book titles
Starter Bear tracks	150–190	16	*Got You!; Pet Day; Where's Blop?; New School*

There are four fiction books at starter level. The books are science fiction and centre around a group of characters at a school on the planet Zap. Most of the teachers and children are aliens and are introduced in *Bear tracks*. The *Bear tracks* book *New School* introduces Nick, an earth boy who is the 'point of view' character for many of the subsequent books.

For *Bear tracks*, the sentence length of the fiction books is typically shorter than those of the non-fiction books, but the pages are designed to show clearly how the meaning of one sentence relates to another. This is because of the particular challenges that narrative fiction books present to the reader, including the fact that stories often involve more abstract ideas and that the readers have to sustain their understanding throughout a whole book. The fiction books have been written with these challenges in mind, and the text and pictures work well together to support the reader in understanding the story.

Picture cues can be helpful in fiction books, but children do need to be able to decode a lot of text without them. For this reason, there is a strong emphasis on the use of phonically regular words and high frequency words in these texts. Content words for each book (e.g. *school, class, teacher*) are indicated on the front cover of the Guided Reading Booklets. These words are often predictable by the context.

Non-fiction

The different non-fiction text types each have their own conventions that children need to become familiar with. The main text word count varies from text type to text type according to the demands of the language as well as the complexity of the layouts, etc. Although there is a progression in the phonics and the high frequency words used in these books, there are also many more 'content words' which are easily readable or predictable in context. As children read these books, they will develop a wide range of reading strategies which include reading on, predicting a word that makes sense, using analogy with other words on the page, reading the pictures, as well as phonic cues and knowledge of high frequency words.

Pictures Whilst highly illustrated picture books are often associated with younger children, pictures are accepted as an integral part of non-fiction books. When reading non-fiction, children who rely heavily on pictures as a cueing strategy do not have to feel concerned about peer reaction to the level of illustration in the book.

Reading strategies While developing phonic and word recognition skills continues to be important, for many of our target readership, the active promotion of text and sentence level reading strategies can be very beneficial. Through the reading of captions and of shorter texts linked to pictures and diagrams, children can be taught to look at reading skills that focus more on monitoring meaning than on decoding individual words.

Non-fiction: report texts

Trackers level	Number of words	Number of pages	Book titles
Starter Bear tracks	60–80	16	*From Rock to Rap* (history of music and fashion); *Working Animals* (jobs that animals do for us)

There are at least two report texts at each level of *Trackers* because reports are the most common non-fiction text type that children are likely to meet in school. In these books, the main text can be quite short, giving just enough information to create a context so that children can understand and interpret the pictures, diagrams, time lines and charts. There are substantial opportunities for adding information through secondary text.

Report texts have the lowest main text word count of the *Trackers* text types. This is because children need to be taught to read and interpret all the information on a spread, including how to use the heading, captions, labels, key, illustrations, diagrams, time lines, etc. Report texts also have more secondary text, adding an extra level of challenge for children who are gaining in confidence. The report texts contain interesting new information that will enrich cross-curricular explorations for the whole class.

Non-fiction: puzzle texts

Trackers level	Number of words	Number of pages	Book titles
Starter Bear tracks	100–150	16	*Stripes and Stars* (visual games with shapes and patterns); *Amazing Mazes* (navigating routes using code)

Interactive puzzle texts are unique to *Trackers*. Visual literacy is developed as children search pictures for clues and interpret them to find answers to questions. These are immediately very motivating books in which the purpose of the reading is apparent – you need to read the text in order to find out what to do!

As children read the puzzle books and do the puzzles, they develop many higher order reading skills such as skimming and scanning, searching for patterns and shapes, logical, methodical thinking, deduction and inference. Main text always gives required information and poses questions. Secondary text can be used to ask additional, more searching questions.

Non-fiction: explanation texts

Trackers level	Number of words	Number of pages	Book titles
Starter Bear tracks	99	16	*How a Skateboard is Made* (how the component parts of a skateboard are assembled)

Explanations of different kinds are commonly encountered. They can sometimes be very 'text heavy' whereas at other times they can be achieved through simple flow diagrams. Explanations which are easiest to understand often combine the two.

There is one explanation text at Starter level. Thereafter, explanations are found in some of the magazine texts at higher levels.

Non-fiction: 'magazine' format books

Trackers level	Number of words	Number of pages	Book titles
Starter Bear tracks	97	16	*What Rots?* (causes, results and types of rot)

The 'magazine' format books include two or three different text types that are related to a common theme. This format gives children the opportunity to recognise that there is more than one way of presenting information. The Guided Reading Booklets give clear indications about the language features of each of the text types included. There is one magazine book at Starter level, and others at further levels in *Trackers*.

Non-fiction: instruction/procedural text
At *Bear tracks*, instructions are specifically taught in the magazine book, *What Rots?*, but are also used for text in the puzzle books. This gives children the experience of reading and using instructions for different purposes and in comparing purposes and layouts. There are instruction texts at every level of *Trackers*.

Structure

The development of skills through *Trackers* is carefully structured to ensure that children make appropriate progress while existing skills are consolidated and made secure. In order to give opportunities for adequate reinforcement, there are a total of 10 books at each level (four fiction and six non-fiction) and seven levels of books to span the reading ages from approximately 5:6 to 7:6.

The level descriptions in the Book Bands reference book (UK Reading Recovery National Network) have been used to give guidance as to text features which are appropriate at each level, but since *Trackers* is aimed at an older target readership, some of the Book Bands level descriptors are inappropriate (for example, we have a greater amount of text on a page; we

have more pages in a book; we have more complex story lines). We have, however, structured the degree of support given to the reader through the development of features such as:

★ consistency of sentence structure and how closely sentence structure reflects spoken language;

★ predictability of story line;

★ relationship between text and pictures;

★ phonic skills necessary to decode phonically regular words;

★ percentage of high frequency, or phonically regular, words.

The following table shows the structured progression within *Trackers* of some of these skills and strategies:

Trackers level	Word count (see also text type descriptions)	Number of pages	Phonic focus	Average sentence length	High frequency words
Starter Bear tracks	60–190	16	CVC words*	4–6	35
1 Elephant tracks	75–400	16	Initial and final consonant blends	5–6 words	+25
2 Frog tracks	150–475	16	Initial and final consonant blends	6 words	+15
3 Giraffe tracks	300–510	16	Introducing common long vowel phonemes	6–7 words	+20
4 Parrot tracks	500–720	24	Consolidating common long vowel phonemes	6–7 words	+30
5 Tiger tracks	620–920	24	Introducing other long vowel phonemes	7+ words	+50
6 Zebra tracks	690–970	24	Consolidating other long vowel phonemes	7+ words	+50

* Note that CVC words are defined as being words made up of three phonemes: consonant, short vowel phoneme, consonant. Although most CVC words are written with three letters, e.g. *cut*, *big*, *fed*, some consonant phonemes are represented by two letters, so words such as *Ship*, *Tizz* and *Shell* are included as CVC words.

★ *Word count and number of pages* The rise in word count and page numbers reflects the expectation that reading stamina and proficiency are developing. The variations of word count within a level are appropriate to the different text types.

★ *Phonic focus* This progression of phonic skills is consistent with that recommended in DfES phonics programmes. The 'phonic focus' does not imply that the books exclusively use words with these letter patterns, but that there is a preponderance of such words where possible. This is particularly apparent in the fiction books.

* *Average sentence length* There is no direct correlation between the difficulty of a text and sentence length, but average sentence length can be an indication of the increasing difficulty of texts. Sometimes, longer sentences are easier to read because they can clarify the relationship between two otherwise unconnected sentences.
* *High frequency words* These are words which are used frequently across all the books in a level. The *Trackers* high frequency words for starter level are listed in the table on page 10.

Trackers level	Cumulative high frequency (H/F) words*
Starter Bear tracks	a, and, are, at, back, but, can, can't, for, get, got, he, him, his, how, I, in, is, it, no, of, on, ran, said, she, stop, the, they, this, to, us, was, went, with, you

* High frequency words are cumulative (i.e. words introduced at one level will continue to be reinforced at the next) and are found in several books at the level. They are largely consistent with words recommended in most high frequency word lists.

Other, less measurable, ways in which *Trackers* books are structured are:
* *Content* The earlier books, both fiction and non-fiction, have cognitively less demanding content than the later books. As the children read through the levels they will encounter increasingly demanding ideas.
* *'Word attack' strategies* In the Guided Reading Booklets for the first levels, fairly simple strategies are suggested which build on familiar strategies children have been developing since they began reading (e.g. sounding out by letter and by syllable).

* *Page design* Although designers always design books individually, there are fewer constraints in the higher levels. This means, for example, that there are some pages that have a lot more text on them than others. This is consistent with other age-appropriate books children will meet in the classroom. The text will, of course, still be very structured, but the books will increasingly look like other books in the class library.
* *Comprehension focus* Different kinds of comprehension are the focus of different questions posed in the Guided Reading Booklets. 'Retrieval of detail' questions are suggested to help children to focus on what they have actually read in the book; 'simple inference' questions encourage children to reflect on what they have read and to draw their own conclusions; and 'personal response' questions ask children to give their opinions and to relate what they have read to their own experiences. As children progress through *Trackers*, more searching questions are suggested that require children to use more inferential and deductive comprehension. These require a greater understanding of the text and challenge children to think much harder about what they have read.

Literacy across the curriculum

Many children who find reading challenging, or who lack confidence in reading, experience independent research as a daunting task, particularly if they have previously been encouraged to engage only at a literal level with text (for example, simply locating information rather than truly understanding it). Finding information independently, however, is a skill that all children need to develop.

Although the texts are accessible, the variety of layouts used in *Trackers* is similar to those used in other non-fiction books. You can use these books to teach age-appropriate information retrieval skills in a range of different text types. Use the non-fiction organisational features to teach children to locate information more efficiently. Features included are:

★ covers, title and blurb
★ contents
★ main text
★ headings and sub-headings
★ captions and labels.

The chart below indicates how the *Trackers* books can be used to support other curriculum areas. *Trackers* have not been written to conform with any particular syllabus, since the emphasis is on the motivational nature of the content and the suitability of the books for different age groups, but many of the books can be linked with cross-curricular work. Since the ideas and information in the *Trackers* books are unlikely to be duplicated by more conventional topic-based library books, the children finding information in *Trackers* will have a unique contribution to make.

Bear tracks	Stripes and Stars	Amazing Mazes	How a Skateboard is made	What Rots?	From Rock to Rap	Working Animals
Maths		Angles; thinking mathematically			*Calculating how long ago*	
Science	*Camouflage*			Bacteria – good or bad? Healthy living		Habitats
ICT		Simple programming: LOGO	Internet and computers in commerce			
Geography	*National Flags*	Planning routes				Climate. Landscape, impact of people on natural areas
History					20th-century history	
Art / Design and technology	Van Gogh	*Opportunities to design and construct own maze*	Making design choices for a purpose		*Responding to different stimuli*	
Music					Responding to music	
RE / PSHCE						Different moralities
Thinking skills	Logical and deductive reasoning	*Logical and deductive reasoning*		Constructing an argument		Constructing an argument

Italics indicates only a passing reference.

Speaking and listening

Some of the children who struggle with reading, particularly those for whom English is an additional or foreign language, are likely to find speaking and listening challenging. This is often because they feel inadequate when faced by their more articulate peers and they don't think that they have a valid contribution to make to a discussion. Encouraging such children to develop their speaking and listening skills is crucial both for their self-esteem and to promote their own intellectual development.

Trackers supports speaking and listening development in a number of key ways:

★ *through group work: Trackers* books can be used in activities that involve children in talking and listening, remembering and summarising specific information. This is less threatening than having to form and offer opinions on the spot.

★ *through the exciting content and design: Trackers* books are designed to be pored over and discussed by pairs of children. The 'social' aspect of reading is part of the rationale for the design and format of the non-fiction books in particular.

★ *through the Reading Booklets:* Each *Trackers* book has a Guided Reading Booklet (see page 14) to accompany it which is full of opportunities to develop ideas and concepts through speaking and listening.

★ *through the photocopiable 'leaflet' on pages 46 and 47 of this Guide:* This gives suggestions for guided reading and about asking and answering questions.

Reading and writing

Many children who experience difficulties with reading also find writing challenging. Although *Trackers* is primarily a reading resource, it also promotes writing development:

★ *by providing good models of texts:* children find it difficult to write different kinds of texts if they are not familiar with the basic conventions and language use of the text type. By providing a wide range of well written texts – albeit using comparatively simple language structures – *Trackers* offers good models on which children can base their own writing.

★ *by scaffolding information gathering techniques:* for each non-fiction *Trackers* book there is a photocopy master (PCM) worksheet which presents a framework for children to find and record information. This activity has a dual purpose: it promotes reading for meaning and information sorting strategies whilst at the same time offering a model for ways in which information can be gathered and recorded as a preparation for writing.

Using *Trackers* in the classroom

Trackers books are intended to be used for three purposes:
1. for children to browse through, enjoy and share with their friends and family;
2. to support cross-curricular classroom projects;
3. for guided reading, supported by either a teacher or a teaching assistant.

Using *Trackers* for guided reading

To support you in using *Trackers* for guided reading, each *Trackers* book is accompanied by:
* pages in this Teacher's Guide that give you information about each book including the blurb, lists of high frequency and 'tricky' words, the phonic focus, useful decoding strategies, suggested cross-curricular links and information about the photocopy master (PCM) worksheets;
* three PCMs for each non-fiction book and two for each fiction book. For all the books, the first PCM addresses word level skills that help to develop reading fluency and accuracy, and the second PCM focuses on reading comprehension. The third non-fiction PCM always scaffolds a writing task based on the book;
* a Guided Reading Booklet.

Guided Reading Booklet

The Guided Reading Booklet can be used by teaching assistants or parent helpers working with a group, pairs or individual pupils. It includes a format for organising guided reading sessions and suggests ways to introduce each book so that the children are more likely to achieve success. There are also discussion points for a final session in which the children consider what they have achieved. For the fiction books, this final section includes comprehension questions that develop SATs-type comprehension skills, focusing on 'finding evidence', 'using inference' and 'personal response'.

In addition, the Guided Reading Booklet gives page by page suggestions, including:
* discussion points to make sure that the children are understanding the progression of the text;
* information about layout. This is particularly useful for the non-fiction books since part of

the skill of information retrieval in non-fiction is understanding how the information is presented;
* ways of introducing and exploring 'tricky' words that are appropriate to the reading strategies being developed.

For each double page spread there is a 'follow on' section. This contains word and sentence level features (e.g. punctuation, style, word choice, fonts used) which children need to understand. It also contains a 'making meaning' feature which encourages children to think around the text on the page, making links to their own experiences or general knowledge and developing inferential comprehension.

Leaflet

More general information about organising guided reading sessions is given in the A5 photocopiable leaflet on pages 46 and 47 of this Guide. This leaflet is written for teaching assistants and parent helpers, and suggests ways of organising a series of sessions around a book. It also explains how asking as well as answering questions can help to develop a child's understanding of a book and motivate them to read.

Home/school links using *Trackers*

Children will enjoy reading *Trackers* so much that they will be keen to take them home to re-read with parents and carers. Depending on your school policy, you may be happy to send the books home, or you may prefer to keep sets intact in school. Either way, the worksheets for each book can make good homework activities. For this reason, at least one of the worksheets for each book can be completed without direct reference to the *Trackers* book (although children will need to have read the *Trackers* book in order to understand the activity).

Which level of *Trackers* should a child be reading?

As you become more familiar with *Trackers*, you will gain a better understanding of how it fits with other reading resources you use, and which children will read most happily at which levels.

The following chart may be helpful:

Trackers level	Associated Book Band level	Approximate National Curriculum level	Scottish 5–14 level	NI Curriculum level
Starter Bear tracks	Yellow	Working within level 1	Working within level A	Working within level 1
1 Elephant tracks	Blue	Working within level 1	Working within level A	Working towards level 2
2 Frog tracks	Green	Working within level 1	Working within level A	Working towards level 2
3 Giraffe tracks	Orange	Working towards level 2	Working towards level B	Working within level 2
4 Parrot tracks	Turquoise	Working towards level 2	Working towards level B	Working within level 2
5 Tiger tracks	Purple	Working within level 2	Working within level B	Working within level 2
6 Zebra tracks	Gold	Working within level 2	Working within level B	Working within level 2

For ease of use in the classroom, note that *Trackers* levels are organised alphabetically. When a child is ready to move on, you don't have to look up the next level – just go to the next one in alphabetical order.

Using the *Trackers* reading profile

Photocopy page 48 and use it to assess children's reading skills and strategies and their knowledge about reading. The *Bear tracks* statements summarise the skills needed to read the *Bear tracks* books, the *Elephant tracks* statements summarise the skills needed to read the *Elephant tracks* books. The statements at each level are not mutually exclusive and it is unlikely that any one of the profiles will exactly match each child. You can use the profile to do a 'best fit' assessment to make initial decisions before trying out *Trackers* at that level.

★ If a child does not know all the letter sounds and struggles to 'sound out' a CVC word, e.g. *bug*, recognises fewer than 30 high frequency words and has difficulty in tracking a text from left to right across a page, then *Trackers* is probably too challenging;

★ If you can tick some, but not all of the *Bear tracks* statements, then the child is probably ready to read *Bear tracks*;

★ If you can tick all the *Bear tracks* and some of the *Elephant tracks* statements, then the child is probably ready to begin reading *Elephant tracks*;

★ If you can tick all the *Bear tracks* and all the *Elephant tracks* statements, then the child may be ready to begin reading *Frog tracks*. (See the relevant *Trackers Teacher's Guide* for the reading profile and information for *Elephant tracks* and *Frog tracks*.)

Stripes and Stars

Stripes and stars are all around us in both natural and manufactured things. All the puzzles in the book feature stripes and stars, so the children need to look carefully to solve them.

Main information about the book

Text type: puzzle	Total number of words: 133	Number of different words: 65
Pictures: illustrations and photographs	Total number of sentences: 17	Average sentence length: 7 words

Trackers high frequency words	'Tricky' words
a, are, for, how, in, is, the, this, you	*between, differences, number, photos, points, United States of America*

Words with CVC	Useful strategies
bit, box, can, cat, fish, fit, had, has, shell, six, ten, that, this, with	Recognising closely related words e.g. *star, starfish; snake, shape*

PCM 1 (p.18) finding rhymes
* Check that the children have a secure understanding of rhyme. Play with words, sounds and non-words to explore rhyming patterns. Read through all the words on the sheet before children start work on it.

PCM 2 (p.19) finding information
* Clarify that you expect the children's drawings to be finished using good observational skills rather than general knowledge. Ask questions to ensure this, e.g. *Are all the zebra's stripes the same width? Which direction do they go in? Are they parallel?*

PCM 3 (p.20) writing a puzzle
* Clarify that the children are not expected to do the puzzle – though they can – but to write instructions so that someone else will know how to do the puzzle.

Amazing Mazes

This book is based on Logo computer programmes. To find their way through the mazes, children have to follow and write Logo codes. These are the same codes used by floor and desktop turtles.

Main information about the book

Text type: puzzle	Total number of words: 106	Number of different words: 55
Pictures: illustrations	Total number of sentences: 23	Average sentence length: 5 words

Trackers high frequency words	'Tricky' words
a, are, at, can, get, how, is, of, on, the, this, to, you	*arrow, code, don't, forward, move, right, rocket, start, write*

Words with CVC	Useful strategies
bat, box, bug, can, cup, get, hit, Jed, put, Sam, shop, tell	Hearing all the sounds in words with a consonant blend, e.g. *left, help, pink*

PCM 1 (p.21) building CVC words
* Help children to follow the code and initially to circle all the letters they land on.
* They should then write the collection of letters (T, C, A, P, I, N, M, S) they have found in the box provided. Some children may also need letters they can manipulate.

PCM 2 (p.22) alphabetical order
* Ask children to write the alphabet on the sheet if they are unsure of the order of the letters.

PCM 3 (p.23) inventing a maze puzzle
* As children design their own version of the game, ask them to explain the choices they are making.

How a Skateboard is Made

This book explains the process of ordering and making a bespoke skateboard.

Main information about the book

Text type: explanation	Total number of words: 99	Number of different words: 46
Pictures: illustrations and diagrams	Total number of sentences: 16	Average sentence length: 6 words

Trackers high frequency words	'Tricky' words
a, at, for, gets, he, him, his, is, on, the, this, with	bearings, board, decks, grip tape, trucks, wants, website, wheels

Words with CVC	Useful strategies
Dad, Dan, deck, get, him, his, man, pick, put, shop, then, with	Hearing all the sounds in words with a consonant blend, e.g. grip, first, next

PCM 1 (p.24) building words
* Check that the children are familiar with all the short vowel sounds 'a', 'e', 'i', 'o', 'u'. Read the words on the skateboards to the children. Can they hear which vowel is in the middle of each word?

PCM 2 (p.25) sequencing events
* Reread the book to the children, discussing the events from Dan's point of view. *What did he do, and in which order?*

* Children cut out the pictures and sequence them on another piece of paper.

PCM 3 (p.26) writing an explanation
* Children may find it helpful to have competed PCM 2 before they do this one, which looks at the other side of the process.

What Rots?

Many things rot – including us, our food and our houses. Sometimes rot is useful to us and sometimes it is harmful. Encourage the children to discuss what they think about rot, when they have read this book.

Main information about the book

Text type: magazine (report and instruction)	Total number of words: 97	Number of different words: 59
Pictures: illustrations and photographs	Total number of sentences: 19	Average sentence length: 5 words

Trackers high frequency words	'Tricky' words
a, and, are, at, but, can, can't, for, in, is, it, the, they, this, you	animals, people, plants, slowly, sweets, teeth, things

Words with CVC	Useful strategies
bad, but, can, put, rot, that, this, wet	Recognising closely related words e.g. rot, rotting; slow, slowly; food, foods

PCM 1 (p.27) high frequency words
* Read through the words in the panel with the children first, to make sure they are familiar with them. Then ask them to write the missing word or words in each sentence.

PCM 2 (p.28) finding information
* Talk through the task with the children before they tackle it. How many different kinds of rot can they remember? They can write these on the circles before they find others in the book.

PCM 3 (p.29) writing instructions
* Reread the instructions in the book together before the children begin this activity. Discuss the layout and features of instruction texts.

From Rock to Rap

Since the 1950s there have been many links between popular music and fashion. This book explores some of them and alerts the children to the possibility of continuing music-related fashions.

Main information about the book

Text type: report Pictures: photographs	Total number of words: 62 Total number of sentences: 8	Number of different words: 40 Average sentence length: 6 words
Trackers high frequency words *and, can, in, is, it, no, on, the, this, to, with, you*		**'Tricky' words** *dance, fashion, hippy, music, punk*
Words with CVC *can, fun, pop, put, rap, rock, sing*		**Useful strategies** Hearing all the sounds in words with a consonant blend, e.g. *fast, glam, punk*

PCM 1 (p.30) words ending with 'ke' or 'ck'
* Discuss the word endings on PCM 1. *What do they both sound like?* Point out the spellings.

PCM 2 (p.31) finding information
* Do children remember which kind of music makes which kind of response? Help them to use the contents page to locate the information.
* Ask the children to look at the clothes and fashions on the pages. Are there colours, shapes and patterns they could associate with more than one type of music? Encourage them to try to represent these beside each of the listed music styles.

PCM 3 (p.32) completing a timeline
* Children will need to use the information in the book to complete the time line, noting the music and drawing sketches to represent the fashions.

Working animals

This book explores some of the ways in which animals work for us. Encourage the children to talk about some of the moral issues involved.

Main information about the book

Text type: report Pictures: photographs and illustrations	Total number of words: 74 Total number of sentences: 15	Number of different words: 39 Average sentence length: 5 words
Trackers high frequency words *are, for, get, in, on, of, they, to, us*		**'Tricky' words** *animals, circuses, coconuts, dolphins, elephants, horses, hospitals, monkeys*
Words with CVC *bug, dog, fish, for, get, job, pull*		**Useful strategies** Recognising plural forms of familiar words: *bugs, dogs, jobs*

PCM 1 (p.33) building words
* Begin by playing with magnetic or wooden letters. Show children how to mix up the letters of a word.
* Develop strategies together for deciding what the word might be, e.g. *Is the vowel likely to go at the beginning of the word?*, *Which pairs of letters are most likely to go together?*, *What sound do they make?*

PCM 2 (p.34) comprehension; writing sentences
* Discuss the features of a sentence. Read through the first question and explore how the answer supplied gives the information requested.

PCM 3 (p.35) recording information
* Talk about how the children can find the information they need efficiently. Check that they know how to use a contents page.
* Note that there might be some discussion about whether the work is good or bad for the animals. Encourage this.

Rhyming words

Write the words that rhyme with 'star' in the starfish.
Write the words that rhyme with 'stripe' in the stripy fish.

Focus: finding rhymes

Shape and patterns

Add the patterns to these pictures.
★ Use the book to find out if you need stars or stripes.
★ Label each picture.
★ Write which page you found it on.

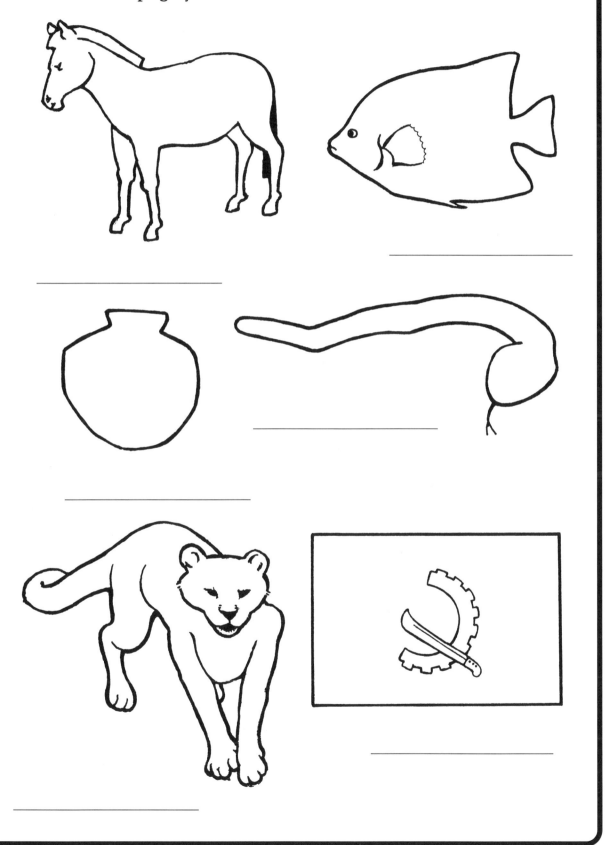

Write what to do

Here is a puzzle. Write what to do to finish the puzzle. (Look in the book for some ideas.)

_____

_____

_____

Now write some questions about the picture.

1 _____

2 _____

3 _____

Focus: writing instructions and questions

Building words

Follow the code and collect the letters you land on.

Write the letters here.

Code
Start
FD 1
RT 90
FD 2

LT 90
FD 1
LT 90
FD 1

FD 2
RT 90
FD 1

FD 1
RT 90
FD 1

LT 90
FD 1
RT 90
FD 1

FD 1
RT 90
FD 2

LT 90
FD 1
LT 90
FD 1

FE 2
End

				e		
	r		a		l	t
Start →				p		u
l		c			i	
	t		n			
b				m		s

How many words can you make using these letters?

Write the words here.

Alphabetical order

Finish the code to land on the letters in alphabetical order.

		b		
a	e			
			d	
		f		
Start ↑	c			g

Start
FD 3

FD 1
RT 90
FD 2

Write out the alphabet.

Focus: alphabetical order

Make your own maze puzzle

Look at the maze on pages 8 and 9.
Draw your own game.

Write the code to get across the maze.

Add the right vowel

Choose a vowel to finish each word.

Find the words in the book and
write which page they are on.

Vowels
a e i o u

D_n _____

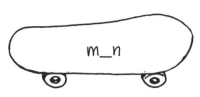
m_n _____

sh_p _____

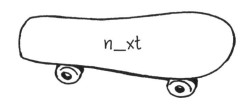
d_ck _____

n_xt _____

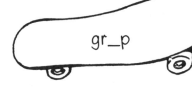
gr_p _____

tr_cks _____

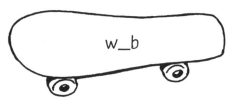
w_b _____

w_th _____

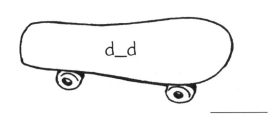
d_d _____

p_ck _____

Focus: building words

The right order

What did Dan do?
★ Cut out the boxes.
★ Put them in the right order.

What do you think Dan did next? Draw and write about it on another piece of paper.

Focus: sequencing events

25

Sequencing words

★ Cut out the boxes.
★ Put them in the right order.
★ Write a sequencing word in each gap to
  show each stage of the explanation.

First   Next   Then   After that   Finally

_____, the man put the trucks on the deck.	_____, Dan sent in his order.
_____, the man got Dan's deck.	_____, the man put the grip tape on Dan's deck.
_____, the man got the bearings.	_____, the man put the wheels on the truck.

Label this diagram of a skateboard.

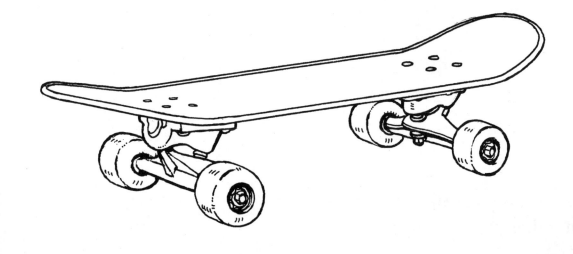

Focus: writing an explanation

High frequency words

Choose a word to fill the gap or gaps in each sentence.

Words to choose from:
and   the   This   can   can't   for   You   They   in

1.   Old food _____ plants rot.

2. They make food _____ new plants.

3. _____ fork is rotting.

4. Animals rot. _____ make food _____ new plants.

5. Sweets _____ fizzy drinks rot teeth.

6. We _____ slow rot down but we _____ stop it.

7. _____ will need:
2 teeth
2 glasses
fizzy drink
tap water.

1) Put _____ drinks _____ the glasses.

Good and bad rot

Some rot is good.

Some rot is bad.

Find ideas from the book about good and bad rot.
Write them in the circles.

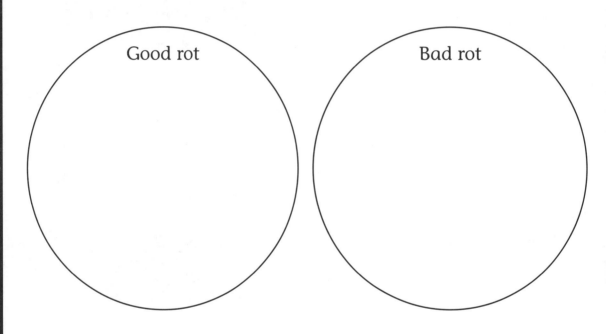

Good rot   Bad rot

Finish these sentences:

Rot is good when _____.

Rot is bad when _____.

Focus: finding information

Writing instructions

Read these notes for writing instructions.

Get:	Then:
teeth	drinks in glasses
glasses	teeth in glasses
drinks	look
water	note

Rewrite the notes as full instructions.

_____

_____

_____

_____

_____

_____

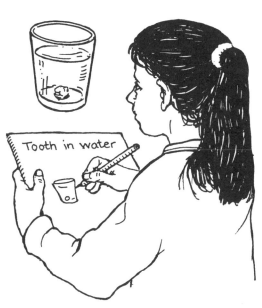

_____

_____

_____

_____

_____

Focus: writing instructions

Word endings

Read the words below. Finish them with <u>ck</u> or <u>ke</u>.

 r o ___ ___

 c a ___ ___

 b a ___ ___

 n e ___ ___

 b i ___ ___

 k i ___ ___

 d u ___ ___

 r a ___ ___

 s o ___ ___

 s a ___ ___

Focus: words ending with 'ke' and 'ck'

Finding information

Match the music with what it makes you want to do.

Pattern	This music	makes you want to...
	Rock 'n' roll	dance.
	Pop	pogo.
	Hippy	rock 'n' roll.
	Punk	say the words – not sing them.
	Glam rock	say 'no more war'.
	Rap	_____ (Write this one yourself.)

Draw a pattern to match each kind of music.

Who are these people?

_____   _____   _____

Making a time line

Finish the time line by:
★ filling in the name of the music
★ drawing the fashion.

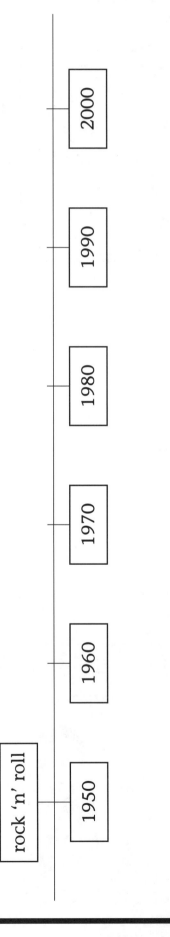

Focus: completing a time line

Sorting letters into words

Work out the words in each set of bubbles.
All the words are in the book.

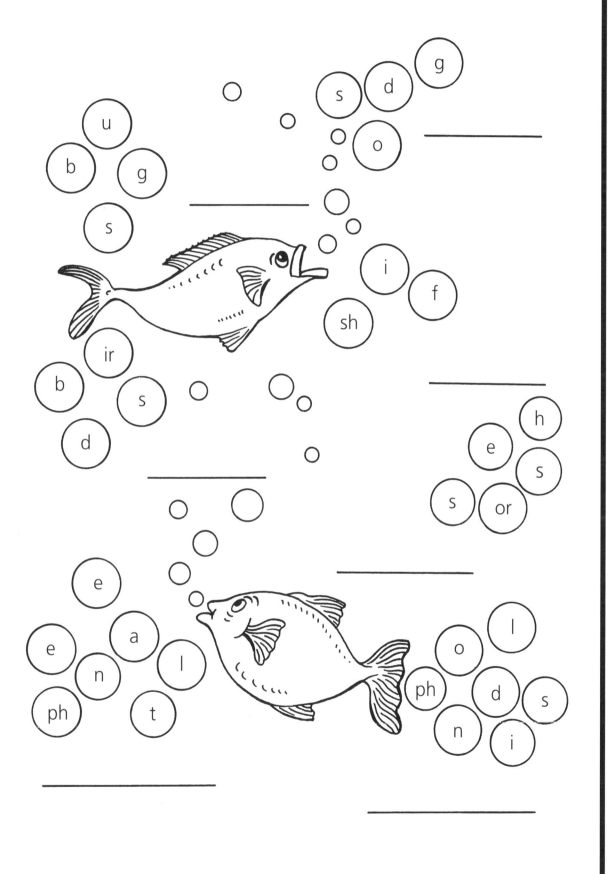

Focus: building words

Which animal?

Find the answer to these questions.
Write them in sentences, like the one below.

Which animal can help the police?

   Dogs can help the police.

Which two animals can carry us?

_____

Which animals catch fish for us?

_____

Which animals get coconuts for us?

_____

Which two animals carry things for us?

_____

Which animals work for us in hospitals?

_____

Which animals find bombs for us?

_____

34   Focus: comprehension; writing sentences

Facts and opinions

Fill in the grid to show how animals work for us.
You can write or draw the answers.

Animal name	The job or jobs they do for us	Good or bad work?
Birds		
Dogs		
Dolphins		
Elephants		
Horses		
Maggots		
Worms		
Add another animal.		
Add another animal.		
Add another animal.		

Tick if you think the work is good.
Cross if you think the work is bad.

Got you!

Slig plays mean tricks on everyone. Tizz and Kaz try to get him back, but they can't until one of Slig's own tricks backfires.

Main information about the book

Total number of words: 166 Total number of sentences: 31	Number of different words: 83 Average sentence length: 5 words
Trackers high frequency words _a, and, but, can't, for, get, got, he, him, his, no, on, ran, said, the, they, to, went, you_	**'Tricky' words** _coming, friends, Glitch, mean, school, Slig, snap, teacher, watched_
Words with CVC _bell, box, but, buzz, get, got, had, hid, his, Kaz, kid, Lug, put, ran, set, shot, Tizz_	**Useful strategies** Hearing all the sounds in words with a consonant blend, e.g. _Slig, snap, went_

PCM 1 (p.38) hearing consonant blends

★ Read the sentences together. Can children work out what the incomplete words should be?
★ Ask one child to read the incomplete word aloud while the other listens. Can they hear the missing consonant each time?
★ Children complete the work independently.

PCM 2 (p.39) comprehension

★ Read the first question together and discuss whether or not it is true. Show the children how to complete the sheet by writing 'yes' if it's a true statement and 'no' if it's not.
★ Encourage the children to check their answers using the book.
★ Suggest to the children that when they write their own sentences, one should be true and the other not.

Pet Day

On Pet Day all the children bring their pets to school. Slig has a vicious pet and he makes fun of everyone else's. But Slig's pet ends up cowering on the floor. Whose pet is responsible?

Main information about the book

Total number of words: 170 Total number of sentences: 35	Number of different words: 88 Average sentence length: 4 words
Trackers high frequency words _a, and, at, he, him, his, I, in, is, it, of, on, ran, said, she, the, this, to, was_	**'Tricky' words** _again, children, claws, could, mouth, school_
Words with CVC _back, big, Fang, fell, fun, get, got, let, lick, lip, mad, pet, put, ran, rock, Rox, Ted, then, Vish, well, will_	**Useful strategies** Recognising that two letters can sometimes be pronounced as one sound, e.g. _ll, ck_

PCM 1 (p.40) finding the medial vowel

★ Ask the children to read the words on PCM 1. Ask them how they work out what the words say. Which sort of letter is missing each time? Check that they are familiar with and understand the word 'vowel' and that they can list the short vowels.
★ Some children may need plastic letters to manipulate in order to explore the possibilities.

PCM 2 (p.41) finding information

★ Read the sentences on the PCM together. Ask children to suggest a suitable additional sentence for the last box.
★ Can all the children match each pet to its owner? Encourage them to use the book to make their drawings accurate.

Where's Blop?

Blop keeps on being late for school. Kaz decides that she will help Blop to get there on time, but when Blop forgets his bag and they miss the school bus, it looks as though Blop will be late again.

Main information about the book

Total number of words: 179 Total number of sentences: 33	Number of different words: 80 Average sentence length: 5 words
Trackers high frequency words *a, and, at, can, can't, for, get, got, he, I, in, is, it, no, of, on, ran, said, she, stop, the, they, this, to, was, went, you*	**'Tricky' words** *again, school, use*
Words with CVC *back, bag, bus, but, can, get, got, had, hit, jet-box, Kaz, Miss, not, ran, run, shop, shot, top, Vish, yes*	**Useful strategies** Hearing all the sounds in words with a consonant blend, e.g. *Blop, left, stop*

PCM 1 (p.42) finding rhyming words.
* ★ Check that the children have a secure concept of rhyme and they can use words, nonsense words and sounds as they explore rhymes.
* ★ Read the words in the box. Can children predict possible rhymes?
* ★ Ask the children to complete the PCM. Check that they understand that when they write rhyming words, they only change the beginning of the word each time.

PCM 2 (p.43) sequencing events from a story
* ★ Look at the PCM together. Ask the children to tell you what's happening in each picture.
* ★ Can they explain the order in which events occurred in the story?
* ★ Ask them to cut the pictures out and stick them onto a piece of paper in order.

New School

Nick and Jen are going to live on the Planet Zap. On the long journey through space, Mum gives them a video to watch about their new school. So why does Jen rush for the escape pod?

Main information about the book

Total number of words: 189 Total number of sentences: 31	Number of different words: 87 Average sentence length: 5 words
Trackers high frequency words *a, and, are, for, he, I, in, is, no, said, the, to, went, with, you*	**'Tricky' words** *button, film, monster, planet, school, watched*
Words with CVC *back, bit, but, did, get, got, had, Jen, job, long, lot, Mum, Nick, not, pod, put, red, ran, run, this*	**Useful strategies** Begin to help children to hear all the sounds in words with a consonant blend, e.g. *jump, stop, trip*

PCM 1 (p.44) making rhyming words
* ★ Check that the children's concept of rhyme is secure and that they can play rhyming games with words, non-words and sounds.
* ★ Look at the sheet together and read the top word in each pair. Encourage the children to complete the rhyming word.

PCM 2 (p.45) comprehension
* ★ Reread the book to the children in order that they have the complete story well established.
* ★ Read the sentence beginnings on the PCM and ask children how they think the sentence should finish. Ask children to repeat the entire sentence each time.

Hear the consonant sounds

Read what the people are saying.
Fill in the missing letters in the words.

S_ig likes to play t_icks.

I put out my ha_d.

I need to go to C_ass 12.

I can he_p you.

Let's p_ay a trick on Slig.

Let's set a t_ap.

I we_t into the class.

The t_ap went S_AP!

Focus: hearing consonant blends

True or not?

Read the sentences. Are they true or not?
Write 'yes' or 'no'.

Slig liked to play tricks.   _____

Tizz liked Slig.   _____

Tizz liked Kaz.   _____

Tizz's hand went BUZZ.   _____

Tizz's hand went SNAP.   _____

Tizz and Kaz set a trap.   _____

Slig helped the new kid.   _____

Slig liked the new kid.   _____

Slig set a trap.   _____

Slig saw the trap.   _____

Write two more sentences about the end of the story.
One should be true, the other not.

_____

_____

_____

_____

Focus: comprehension

The right vowel

Fill in the missing vowels.

a e i o u

p_t

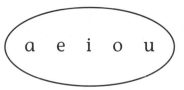

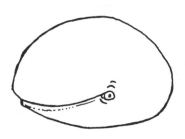

R_x

T_d

V_sh

b_g

Choose one of the vowels
to complete these words.

m__d   l_t

l_p   p__t

r__n

th__n

w__ll

Focus: finding the medial vowel

Pets and owners

★ Read the sentences in each box.
★ Write the missing names.
★ Draw the right pet beside each box.

_____ is Slig's pet. He is strong and fast.	
_____ is Blop's pet. She jumped on Fang.	
_____ is Vish's pet.	

Write another sentence about Ted.

_____

Focus: finding information

Find the rhyme

Draw a line from each word to a picture that rhymes with it.

_____ _____ _____

```
ran    top
    box
not    run
    bag
jet    back
```

_____ _____

_____ _____ _____

Label the pictures.

Focus: finding rhyming words

The right order

Number the pictures in the right order.

☐ (This is fast!)   ☐ (We'll have to run.)

☐ (STOP!)   ☐ (You can't be late.)

Draw what happened next.

Rhyming words

Write a word that rhymes with each word from the story.

had
m_____

lot
p_____

Zap
c_____

not
d_____

did
ki_____

ran
p_____

pod
n_____

red
b_____

Draw pictures for the words you have written.
Can you think of another rhyming word for each set?

Focus: making rhyming words

Finishing sentences

Choose an ending to finish each sentence.

Beginnings

Nick and Jen went to Zap because

Nick watched a lot of films because

Jen went out because

Nick ran after Jen because

The pod stopped because

Jen ran away because

Endings

Mum had a new job.

Jen ran to the exit pod.

Jen hit the red button.

she wanted a snack.

she saw monsters at the new school.

the trip to Zap was very long.

Focus: comprehension

45

Using *Trackers* in guided reading

Guided reading

This is the term used to describe a session in which an adult works for about 20–25 minutes with a group of up to six children, all reading the same book.

A guided reading session should have four distinct parts:

- Introduction (2–3 minutes)
- Independent reading with a purpose (10–12 minutes)
- Returning to the text (5–6 minutes)
- Conclusion (2–3 minutes).

The Guided Reading Booklet for each individual *Trackers* book has more detailed suggestions, but this leaflet aims to explain the purpose of each part of the guided reading session and to offer ideas for good practice during the session.

Introduction

This may vary according to whether this is the first session with the book or a follow-up session.

In the **first session**, the purpose is to introduce the book.

- Identify the teaching and learning objectives of the session.
- Introduce the book by:
  - using the title, blurb and cover illustrations to predict the subject matter and text type;
  - finding out what children already know about the subject.
- Remind children of recently introduced reading strategies.
- Agree on questions to be resolved during independent reading.

Asking and answering questions

There is a real skill to asking and answering questions in order to establish the child's true understanding both of the subject matter they are reading and of the reading strategies. There are two basic question types:

Closed questions are questions to which there is only one correct answer. An example might be: *Which planet is nearest to the sun? What sound does 'dog' begin with?*

Closed questions can be used to check whether or not a child knows or has found out a certain 'fact', but they don't usually show whether or not a child has understood something.

Open questions are questions to which there are many possible answers. Examples are questions which begin: *Why do you think . . .? In your opinion . . .? How would you . . .?*

Open questions are much better for assessing how much a child understands. They are also useful starting points for discussion, because different children may have different opinions.

Children asking questions

Encourage children to ask questions. By asking questions, children can begin to feel a sense of ownership of their own knowledge and understanding, and it gives them more control over what they need to know. Useful strategies in answering children's questions include:

- giving the child an opportunity to phrase the question accurately;
- when possible, encouraging other children to answer the questions;
- asking the questioner what s/he thinks may be the answer;
- trying to answer the question in a way that relates to the child's existing knowledge.

In the **follow-up session**, the purpose of the introduction is to re-focus the children on the book and to establish questions for further discussion.

- Identify the teaching objective of the session.
- Ask the children what they remember about the book from the previous session. Ask them to find parts of the text that gave specific information.
- Recall recently introduced reading strategies (e.g. *What can you do if you get stuck on a word? What should you do if you know that you have lost the sense of the passage?*).
- Identify points of possible difficulty (e.g. *Can you all find the word at the beginning of page 5? How could we work out what the word says?*). Many of these possible 'tricky' words are identified in the Guided Reading Booklet for the individual books.
- Agree on questions that the children are going to resolve during the independent reading part of the session. These are often suggested in the Guided Reading Booklet.

Independent reading

In this part of the session, the children should read the specified section of the book and try to resolve the agreed questions. As far as possible, the children should be encouraged to work independently. Meanwhile you can:

- sample the children's reading by listening carefully to short passages read by each one. Make careful use of specific praise, e.g. for strategies chosen or for phrasing and fluency;
- support individual readers (who are struggling) using selected prompts, if possible making reference to reading strategies discussed earlier.

Returning to the text

This is an important part of the session, because it is here that you can establish what the children understood from their reading. Use it to:

- ask the whole group if they were aware of any problems they encountered. Encourage group involvement in solving the problem;
- agree answers to the questions posed earlier;
- ask children to summarise what they have read;
- ask children to explain reading strategies they used and praise their use of emerging strategies;
- ask additional questions to prompt successful problem-solving strategies (e.g. *How did you know how to say this word? How did you decide which bit of the text was important to read?*);
- ask further questions to probe more deeply into the children's understanding of what they read;
- demonstrate effective reading by re-reading a section of the text yourself.

Conclusion

This part of the session can be used to:

- ask for personal responses to the text (e.g. *What do you remember best? Which bit interested you the most?*);
- establish questions for a future session with the same *Trackers* book;
- summarise the reading strategies that have been effective;
- return to the teaching and learning objectives to establish whether they have been achieved.

Reading profile for *Bear tracks* and *Elephant tracks*

Child's name_____   Assessment date _____

Home language _____   Date of birth _____

Reading for meaning

Bear tracks
- rereads a simple book, retaining the overall meaning?   YES/ NO
- with help, can read simple sentences?   YES/ NO
- remembers character names and reads them correctly next time they appear?   YES/ NO
- uses some features of a word to 'guess' what the word says, not always accurately?   YES/ NO

Elephant tracks
- expects the text to make sense?   YES/ NO
- predicts a word using syntactic cues?   YES/ NO
- predicts a word using picture cues?   YES/ NO
- has a general sense of 'what has been read so far'?   YES/ NO
- expresses an opinion about what has been read?   YES/ NO

Reading for information

Bear tracks
- uses pictures to identify the main topic?   YES/ NO
- can link what is already known to the topic of a book?   YES/ NO
- can talk about pictures and attempt to find new information in the writing?   YES/ NO

Elephant tracks
- predicts the contents of a book using cover information?   YES/ NO
- can talk about prior knowledge of the main topic in a non-fiction book?   YES/ NO
- uses pictures for information?   YES/ NO

Phonic skills

Bear tracks
- accurate, consistent recognition of all letter sounds?   YES/ NO
- can identify words that 'begin with' each of the common sounds?   YES/ NO
- hears all three sounds in a CVC word?   YES/ NO
- knows that initial letter sound can be used to predict a word?   YES/ NO

Elephant tracks
- reads and writes CVC words?   YES/ NO
- uses phonic knowledge to recognise an initial letter?   YES/ NO
- makes accurate and consistent use of letter sounds to confirm words?   YES/ NO

High frequency words

Bear tracks
- 35 words   YES/ NO

Elephant tracks
- 50 words   YES/ NO
- recognises high frequency words in running text?   YES/ NO
- shows awareness of patterns in words?   YES/ NO